Learn to Read Bulgarian in 5 Days

PAVEL VITKOV

Copyright © 2016

Published by Wolfedale Press 2016

WOLFEDALE PRESS

All rights reserved. No part of this publication may be reproduced, distributed, or transmitted in any form or by any means, including photocopying, recording, or other electronic or mechanical methods, without the prior written permission of the publisher.

The cover image of The Sofia University in Sofia, Bulgaria by: Wengen

ISBN-13: 978-0-9959305-6-8

CONTENTS

Introduction	i
Unit 1 – а, о, к, м, т	1
Unit 2 – у, р, с, в	3
Unit 3 – и, н, х, б	7
Unit 4 – л, п, д, з	9
Unit 5 – ш, г, ч, й	11
Unit 6 – ъ, ц, ж	13
Unit 7 – я, ю, щ	15
Unit 8 – ф, ь	17
Unit 9 – Review	19
Bulgarian Alphabet	21
Glossary – Thematic Order	23
Glossary – Alphabetical Order	31

INTRODUCTION

Learning a new alphabet can be very intimidating for an English speaker only used to reading the Latin alphabet. This is partly why English speakers tend to stick to learning other languages that use the same alphabet, such as French, Spanish and Italian – because they seem a lot easier!

But learning a new alphabet does not have to be so difficult. The difficulty is finding a good system to learn the new alphabet so that you don't get discouraged and give up before you make real progress.

The secret to learning a new alphabet is to be taught how to pronounce each letter separately, and then to practice how the new letters combine with letters you already know to read real words in the alphabet in a structured way. This is not revolutionary – it is probably how you learned to read English – but it is not easy to find for other languages.

This book will teach you how to read the Bulgarian alphabet in exactly that way, and with this method you will be able to read Bulgarian in only 5 days or less! After that you will be able to enjoy the Bulgarian language and culture in a way that you were never able to before.

THE BULGARIAN ALPHABET
Българска азбука

The Bulgarian language uses 30 letters of the Cyrillic alphabet and is written from left to right. It uses the same basic alphabet as several other Slavic languages, including Russian, Ukrainian and Serbian, although there are differences in pronunciation between Bulgarian and other languages that use the Cyrillic alphabet, just like there are differences in pronunciation between French, Spanish and English even though they use the same alphabet.

Although it does not closely resemble the Latin alphabet used to write English (and other European languages) it is not a difficult alphabet to learn to read. This is because, for the most part, letters are pronounced as they are written and written as they are pronounced, unlike languages such as English that make use of a lot of silent letters and historical spellings. Although correct Bulgarian pronunciation can be difficult for English speakers, learning to read the alphabet is not as much as a challenge as it at first seems.

Like the Latin alphabet used to write English, the Bulgarian alphabet has both upper and lower case letters. Upper case letters are used at the beginning of a sentence and in proper nouns.

HOW TO USE THIS COURSE

The primary goal of this course book is to teach the reader to recognize the Bulgarian alphabet and to begin to read the Bulgarian language.

The main way this is accomplished is by teaching the individual pronunciations of each letter, and then utilizing "Practice" sections where the student can practice reading real Bulgarian words. These "Practice" sections are very important and the main way the student will start to feel comfortable with the Bulgarian alphabet. The answers to all "Practice" questions are included directly below the questions, but try to avoid looking at the answers until you have attempted to answer the questions yourself.

Throughout the book, the reader will also learn approximately 150 real Bulgarian words. These words have been carefully selected to be of maximum benefit to beginner students of the language and are a great starting point for students who want to continue their study of Bulgarian. In the end of the book there are two glossaries – one in thematic order and one in alphabetical order – where the student can study and memorize all the words learned in this course.

The course material has been designed to be completed slowly over 5 days, while reviewing lessons as necessary. You are encouraged to go at whatever pace you feel comfortable with and to feel free to go back to lessons to review as much as needed.

Good luck and I hope you enjoy the first step on your journey to learning the Bulgarian language.

UNIT 1 - а, е, о, к, м, т

The first 6 letters introduced in this course are the letters in Bulgarian that resemble English letters and are pronounced roughly the same. Basically you already know these six Bulgarian letters!

The letter а in Bulgarian is pronounced like the "a" sound in the English words "spa" or "father" (IPA: /a/). The uppercase form is А.

The letter е is pronounced like the "e" sound in the English word "bet" (IPA: /ɛ/). The uppercase form is Е.

The letter о is pronounced like the "o" sound in the English word "hope" (IPA: /o/). The uppercase form is О.

The letter к is pronounced like the "k" sound in the English words "kick" or "kite" (IPA: /k/). The uppercase form is К.

The letter м is pronounced like the "m" sound in the English words "mother" or "Michael" (IPA: /m/). The uppercase form is М.

The letter т is pronounced like the "t" sound in the English words "tan" or "Tom" (IPA: /t/). The uppercase form is Т.

As you can see these 6 letters are virtually the same as in English!

PRACTICE

Try to recognize these English words in their Bulgarian disguises. The answers are below.
1. ат
2. мет
3. кат
4. так
5. кот
6. мат
7. мама

ANSWERS

1. at
2. met
3. cat
4. tack
5. cot
6. mat
7. mama

UNIT 2 - у, р, с, в

The four letters introduced in this unit look like English letters, but unlike Unit 1 these letters are not pronounced the same as in English. Pay close attention to these letters when reading Bulgarian, as their similarity to letters in English make them an easy source of confusion.

The letter у is pronounced like the "oo" sound in "boot", or the end of the word "shoe". (IPA: /u/). It is not pronounced like the "y" sound in the English words "yellow" or "tiny". The pronunciation will be represented by "u" in this book. The uppercase form is У.

The letter р is pronounced like the "r" sound in "restaurant" (IPA: /r/). Although this letter resembles an English "p" it is not pronounced with a "p" sound. The uppercase form is Р.

The letter с is pronounced like the "s" sound in "some" or "same" (IPA: /s/). Although it resembles an English "c", it is never pronounced like the "c" in "cat". It is always pronounced with an "s" sound. The hard "c" sound is spelled with к in Bulgarian. The uppercase form is С.

The letter в is pronounced like the "v" sound in "very" (IPA: /v/). Although this letter resembles an uppercase "B", it is never pronounced like the English "b" sound in "boy". The uppercase form is В.

PRACTICE

Try to recognize these English words in their Bulgarian disguises. Focus on the correct pronunciation and not necessarily the English spelling. The answers are below.

1. рат
2. сат
3. рум
4. катс
5. мотор
6. вет
7. тум
8. васт
9. стов
10. сторм

ANSWERS

1. rat
2. sat
3. room
4. cats
5. motor
6. vet
7. tomb
8. vast
9. stove
10. storm

PRACTICE 2

Try to read these real Bulgarian words. The English translation is given next to each word. The correct pronunciations are given in the answers below.

1. маса   (table)
2. котка   (cat)
3. татко   (dad / daddy)
4. врата   (door)
5. око   (eye)
6. утре   (tomorrow)
7. месо   (meat)

ANSWERS 2

1. masa
2. kotka
3. tatko
4. vrata
5. oko
6. utre
7. meso

UNIT 3 - и, н, х, б

The Bulgarian letter и, which looks like an uppercase "N" written backwards, is pronounced like the "ee" sound in "bee" or the "i" sound in "spaghetti" (IPA: /i/). The pronunciation will be represented by "i" in this book. The uppercase form is И.

The Bulgarian letter н is pronounced like the "n" sound in "now" or "hen" (IPA: /n/). Pay close attention to this letter as it resembles an uppercase "H" in English, but should not be pronounced with an "h" sound. The uppercase form is Н.

The pronunciation of the Bulgarian letter х does not exist in English. It is the "ch" sound in the German "doch" or the "j" sound in the Spanish "ojos". It is a heavy throat clearing "h" sound (IPA: /x/). The pronunciation will be represented by "kh" in this book. The uppercase form is Х.

The letter б is pronounced like the "b" sound in "best" (IPA: /b/). Pay close attention to the letters б and в. The letter б, which looks like the number "6" is pronounced "b" and the letter в, which looks like an uppercase "B", is pronounced "v". With some practice this will become easier. The uppercase form is Б.

THE ACCENT IN BULGARIAN

Like English, in Bulgarian to pronounce a word correctly one must stress one syllable over the others. Also like English, the accent in Bulgarian is not normally written. Think about the English word conduct. It can be pronounced CONduct, or conDUCT although the written language does not tell us which one is correct. This is the same as the situation in Bulgarian.

In Bulgarian-English dictionaries you will often see an accent written on the vowel that is to be stressed in the Bulgarian word. These accents, however, are not normally written in the language and therefore will not be included in the Bulgarian words in this book. However, in order to learn to pronounce the Bulgarian words correctly, the accents will be written in the pronunciation sections of this book.

PRACTICE

Try to read these real Bulgarian words. The English translation is given next to each word. The correct pronunciations (with accents) are given in the answers below.

1. вино (wine)
2. ухо (ear)
3. три (three)
4. нос (nose)
5. банка (bank)
6. брат (brother)
7. храна (food)
8. бира (beer)

ANSWERS

1. víno
2. ukhó
3. tri
4. nos
5. banka
6. brat
7. khraná
8. bíra

UNIT 4 - л, п, д, з

The Bulgarian letter л is pronounced like the "l" sound in "little" or "like" (IPA: /l/). The uppercase form is Л.

The letter п is pronounced like the "p" sound in "pie" or "pepper" (IPA: /p/). The Bulgarian letter resembles the Greek letter pi that you probably remember from geometry. This is not a coincidence as the Cyrillic alphabet derives from the Greek alphabet and some letters are very similar. The uppercase form is П.

The letter д is pronounced like the "d" sound in "dad" (IPA: /d/). The uppercase form is Д.

The letter з is pronounced like the "z" sound in "zoo" (IPA: /z/). This letter resembles the numeral "3". The uppercase form is З.

PRACTICE

Try to read these Bulgarian words. The English translation is given next to each word. The correct pronunciations are given in the answers below.

1. да   (yes)
2. лодка   (boat)
3. стол   (chair)
4. парк   (park)
5. пазар   (market)
6. риза   (shirt)
7. брада   (beard)
8. зелен   (green)

ANSWERS

1. da
2. lódka
3. stol
4. park
5. pazár
6. ríza
7. bradá
8. zelén

UNIT 5 - ш, г, ч, й

The Bulgarian letter ш is pronounced like the "sh" sound in "short" (IPA: /ʃ/). Although written with two letters in English, it is really one sound and it is written with one letter in Bulgarian. This letter will be represented in this book by š. The uppercase form is Ш.

The letter г is pronounced like the "g" sound in "good" (IPA: /g/). The uppercase form is Г.

The letter ч is pronounced like the "ch" sound in "church" (IPA: /tʃ/). Although written with two letters in English, it is really a single sound and is only written with one letter in Bulgarian. This letter will be represented in the pronunciations by č. The uppercase form is Ч.

The letter й is pronounced like the "y" sound in "toy", i.e. it creates a rising diphthong out of the preceding vowel (IPA: /j/). The letter й consists of the letter и with a breve above it, but it is a separate letter in Bulgarian. It will be represented as either an "i" or a "y" in this book after another vowel to attempt to represent the pronunciation without causing confusion. The uppercase form is Й.

PRACTICE

Try to read these Bulgarian words. The English translation is given next to each word. The correct pronunciations are given in the answers below.

1. мишка   (mouse)
2. град   (city)
3. куче   (dog)
4. човек   (person)
5. майка   (mother)
6. лош   (bad)
7. шест   (six)
8. година   (year)
9. чай   (tea)
10. вчера   (yesterday)

ANSWERS

1. míška
2. grad
3. kúče
4. čovék
5. máyka
6. loš
7. šest
8. godína
9. čai
10. včéra

UNIT 6 - ъ, ц, ж

The letter ъ is pronounced like the "u" sound in "turn" (IPA: /ɤ/) or like the "u" sound in "nut" (IPA: /ɐ/). The "u" sound in "Bulgarian" uses this sound in English and sounds similar to the Bulgarian pronunciation of the letter. This letter will be represented as ă in the pronunciation sections of this book. The uppercase form is Ъ.

The letter ц is pronounced like the "ts" sound in "cats" (IPA: /ts/). This is really two sounds, a "t" sound followed by an "s" sound, but it is written with only one letter in Bulgarian. When writing Bulgarian words in English this letter is often represented by a "c", but in this book "ts" will be used in order to avoid confusion with the English "c" sound. Unlike English, in Bulgarian this letter can be used at the beginning of a word and is still pronounced "ts". The uppercase form is Ц.

The letter ж is pronounced like the "s" sound in "pleasure" or "measure" (IPA: /ʒ/). This letter will be represented in this book as ž. The uppercase form is Ж.

PRACTICE

Try to read these Bulgarian words. The English translation is given next to each word. The correct pronunciations are given in the answers below.

1. ръка (hand / arm)
2. кръв (blood)
3. лице (face)
4. сърце (heart)
5. жълт (yellow)
6. дъжд (rain)
7. слънце (sun)
8. месец (month)
9. петък (Friday)
10. четвъртък (Thursday)
11. мъж (man)
12. жена (woman)

ANSWERS

1. răká
2. krăv
3. litsé
4. sărtsé
5. žălt
6. dăžd
7. slăntse
8. mésets
9. petăk
10. četvărtăk
11. măž
12. žená

UNIT 7 - я, ю, щ

The letter я is pronounced like the "ya" sound in "yard" (IPA: /ja/). This letter will be represented in the pronunciation by "ya". This letter looks like a backwards capital "R". The uppercase form is Я.

The letter ю is pronounced like "you", i.e. a "y" sound followed by a "u" (IPA: /ju/). The uppercase form is Ю

The letter щ is pronounced with a "sh" sound followed by a "t" sound, like in the word "shtick". (IPA: /ʃt/). This letter will be written št in the pronunciation in this book. The uppercase form is Щ. Try not to confuse the letter щ with the letter ш that we learned in Unit 5. Notice that щ has a small tail to the right side of the letter.

PRACTICE

Try to read these Bulgarian words. The English translation is given next to each word. The correct pronunciations are given in the answers below.

1. България   (Bulgaria)
2. януари   (January)
3. юни   (June)
4. юли   (July)
5. баща   (father)
6. летище   (airport)
7. рокля   (dress)
8. горещ   (hot)

ANSWERS

1. bǎlgáriya
2. yanuari
3. yúni
4. yúli
5. baštá
6. letište
7. róklya
8. gorešt

UNIT 8 - ф, ь

The final two letters in this course are relatively rare in modern Bulgarian.

The letter ф is pronounced like the "f" sound in "far" (IPA: /f/). The uppercase form is Ф. This letter is mostly used in loanwords from other languages as well as some proper nouns.

The letter ь is rarely seen in Bulgarian; it is only used before the letter о and modifies the "о" sound to "yo", like in the English "yoghurt". This letter is common in other Slavic languages, like Russian for example, but much more rarely used in Bulgarian.

PRACTICE

Try to read these Bulgarian words that have been borrowed from English. Try to guess the pronunciation and the English word. The answers are below.

1. кафе   (coffee)
2. София   (Sofia)
3. февруари   (February)
4. шофьор   (driver)
5. сервитьор   (server)

ANSWERS

1. kafé
2. sofíya
3. fevruari
4. šofyór
5. servítyor

UNIT 9 - REVIEW

PRACTICE 1

Review the previous lessons by reading these real Bulgarian place names below. The correct pronunciations are given in the answers below.
1. Пловдив
2. Варна
3. Стара Загора
4. Благоевград
5. Черно море
6. Област Кюстендил
7. Атанасовско езеро
8. Бургаско езеро
9. Осоговска планина
10. Дяволска река

ANSWERS 1

1. Plovidv
2. Varna
3. Stara Zagora
4. Blagoevgrad
5. Černo More (Black Sea)
6. Oblast Kyustendil
7. Atanasovsko Ezero
8. Burgasko Ezero
9. Osogovska Planina
10. Dyavolska Reka ("Devil's River")

PRACTICE 2

Review what you have learned in this book by reading the Bulgarian names below. The correct pronunciations are given in the answers below.
1. Росен Плевнелиев
2. Бойко Борисов
3. Георги Първанов
4. Димитър Димов
5. Петър Младенов
6. Константин Димитров
7. Корнелия Нинова
8. Вера Мутафчиева

ANSWERS 2

1. Rosen Plevneliev
2. Boyko Borisov
3. Georgi Pǎrvanov
4. Dimitǎr Dimov
5. Petǎr Mladenov
6. Konstantin Dimitrov
7. Korneliya Ninova
8. Vera Mutafčieva

BULGARIAN ALPHABET

Uppercase	Lowercase	Pronunciation
А	а	[a]
Б	б	[b]
В	в	[v]
Г	г	[g]
Д	д	[d]
Е	е	[e]
Ж	ж	[ž]
З	з	[z]
И	и	[i]
Й	й	[y]
К	к	[k]
Л	л	[l]
М	м	[m]
Н	н	[n]
О	о	[o]

П	П	[p]
Р	Р	[r]
С	С	[s]
Т	Т	[t]
У	У	[u]
Ф	Ф	[f]
Х	Х	[kh]
Ц	Ц	[ts]
Ч	Ч	[č]
Ш	Ш	[š]
Щ	Щ	[št]
Ъ	Ъ	[ă]
Ь	Ь	[y]
Ю	Ю	[yu]
Я	Я	[ya]

GLOSSARY – THEMATIC ORDER

ANIMALS

животно	[živótno]	animal
куче	[kúče]	dog
котка	[kótka]	cat
риба	[ríba]	fish
птица	[ptítsa]	bird
крава	[kráva]	cow
свиня	[svinyá]	pig
мишка	[míška]	mouse
кон	[kon]	horse

PEOPLE

човек	[covék]	person
майка	[máyka]	mother
мама	[mama]	mommy / mama
баща	[baštá]	father
татко	[tátko]	daddy / papa
син	[sin]	son
дъщеря	[dǎšteryá]	daughter
брат	[brat]	brother
сестра	[sestrá]	sister
приятел	[priyátel]	friend
мъж	[mǎž]	man
жена	[žená]	woman
момче	[momčé]	boy
момиче	[momiče]	girl
дете	[deté]	child

TRANSPORTATION

влак	[vlak]	train
самолет	[samolét]	airplane
автомобил	[avtomobíl]	car (automobile)
велосипед	[velosipéd]	bicycle
автобус	[avtóbus]	bus
лодка	[lódka]	boat

LOCATION

град	[grad]	city
къща	[kǎšta]	house
улица	[ulitsa]	street
летище	[letište]	airport
хотел	[khotel]	hotel
ресторант	[restorant]	restaurant
училище	[učílište]	school
университет	[universitét]	university
парк	[park]	park
магазин	[magazín]	store / shop
болница	[bólnitsa]	hospital
църква	[tsǎrkva]	church
държава	[dǎržáva]	country (state)
банка	[banka]	bank
пазар	[pazár]	market

HOME

маса	[mása]	table
стол	[stol]	chair
прозорец	[prozórets]	window
врата	[vratá]	door
книга	[kníga]	book

CLOTHING

облекло	[oblekló]	clothing
шапка	[šápka]	hat
рокля	[róklya]	dress
риза	[ríza]	shirt
панталони	[pantaloni]	pants
обувка	[obuvka]	shoe

BODY

тяло	[tyálo]	body
глава	[glavá]	head
лице	[litsé]	face
коса	[kosá]	hair
око	[okó]	eye
уста	[ustá]	mouth
нос	[nos]	nose
ухо	[ukhó]	ear
ръка	[răká]	hand / arm
крак	[krak]	foot / leg
сърце	[sărtsé]	heart
кръв	[krăv]	blood

кост	[kost]	bone
брада	[bradá]	beard

MISCELLANEOUS

да	[da]	yes
не	[ne]	no

FOOD & DRINK

храна	[khraná]	food
месо	[mesó]	meat
хляб	[khlyab]	bread
сирене	[sírene]	cheese
ябълка	[yabǎlka]	apple
вода	[vodá]	water
бира	[bíra]	beer
вино	[víno]	wine
кафе	[kafé]	coffee
чай	[čai]	tea
мляко	[mlyáko]	milk
закуска	[zakúska]	breakfast
обяд	[obyád]	lunch
вечеря	[večérya]	dinner

COLORS

цвят	[tsvyat]	color
червен	[červén]	red
син	[sin]	blue
зелен	[zelén]	green

жълт	[žǎlt]	yellow
черен	[céren]	black
бяло	[byalo]	white

NATURE

море	[more]	sea
река	[reká]	river
езеро	[ézero]	lake
планина	[planiná]	mountain
дъжд	[dǎžd]	rain
сняг	[snyag]	snow
дърво	[dǎrvó]	tree
цвят	[tsvyat]	flower
слънце	[slǎntse]	sun
луна	[luná]	moon
вятър	[vyátǎr]	wind
небе	[nebé]	sky
огън	[ógǎn]	fire
лед	[led]	ice

ADJECTIVES

голям	[golyám]	big
малък	[málǎk]	small
добър	[dobǎr]	good
лош	[loš]	bad
горещ	[gorešt]	hot
студен	[studén]	cold
евтин	[évtin]	cheap
скъп	[skǎp]	expensive

щастлив	[štastlív]	happy
тъжен	[tǎžen]	sad

NUMBERS

едно	[edno]	one
две	[dve]	two
три	[tri]	three
четири	[čétiri]	four
пет	[pet]	five
шест	[šest]	six
седем	[sedem]	seven
осем	[ósem]	eight
девет	[dévet]	nine
десет	[déset]	ten

TIME

ден	[den]	day
месец	[mésets]	month
година	[godína]	year
час	[čas]	hour
днес	[dnes]	today
утре	[utre]	tomorrow
вчера	[včéra]	yesterday

DAYS OF THE WEEK

неделя	[nedelya]	Sunday
понеделник	[ponedelnik]	Monday
вторник	[vtornik]	Tuesday
сряда	[sryáda]	Wednesday
четвъртък	[četvărtăk]	Thursday
петък	[petăk]	Friday
събота	[săbota]	Saturday

MONTHS

януари	[yanuari]	January
февруари	[fevruari]	February
март	[mart]	March
април	[april]	April
май	[mai]	May
юни	[yúni]	June
юли	[yúli]	July
август	[ávgust]	August
септември	[septémvri]	September
октомври	[oktomvri]	October
ноември	[noémvri]	November
декември	[dekembri]	December

PROPER NAMES

България	[bălgáriya]	Bulgaria
български	[bălgarski]	Bulgarian
София	[sofíya]	Sofia

GLOSSARY – ALPHABETICAL ORDER

– A a –

август	[ávgust]	August
автобус	[avtóbus]	bus
автомобил	[avtomobíl]	car (automobile)
април	[april]	April

– Б б –

банка	[banka]	bank
баща	[baštá]	father
бира	[bíra]	beer
болница	[bólnitsa]	hospital
брада	[bradá]	beard
брат	[brat]	brother
България	[bǎlgáriya]	Bulgaria
български	[bǎlgarski]	Bulgarian
бяло	[byalo]	white

– В в –

велосипед	[velosipéd]	bicycle
вечеря	[večérya]	dinner
вино	[víno]	wine
влак	[vlak]	train
вода	[vodá]	water
врата	[vratá]	door
вторник	[vtornik]	Tuesday

| вчера | [včéra] | yesterday |
| вятър | [vyátăr] | wind |

– Г г –

глава	[glavá]	head
година	[godína]	year
голям	[golyám]	big
горещ	[gorešt]	hot
град	[grad]	city

– Д д –

да	[da]	yes
две	[dve]	two
девет	[dévet]	nine
декември	[dekembri]	December
ден	[den]	day
десет	[déset]	ten
дете	[deté]	child
днес	[dnes]	today
добър	[dobăr]	good
дъжд	[dăžd]	rain
дърво	[dărvó]	tree
държава	[dăržáva]	country (state)
дъщеря	[dăšteryá]	daughter

– E e –

евтин	[évtin]	cheap
едно	[edno]	one
езеро	[ézero]	lake

– Ж ж –

жена	[žená]	woman
животно	[živótno]	animal
жълт	[žǎlt]	yellow

– З з –

закуска	[zakúska]	breakfast
зелен	[zelén]	green

– К к –

кафе	[kafé]	coffee
книга	[kníga]	book
кон	[kon]	horse
коса	[kosá]	hair
кост	[kost]	bone
котка	[kótka]	cat
крава	[kráva]	cow
крак	[krak]	foot / leg
кръв	[krǎv]	blood
куче	[kúče]	dog
къща	[kǎšta]	house

– Л л –

лед	[led]	ice
летище	[letište]	airport
лице	[litsé]	face
лодка	[lódka]	boat
лош	[loš]	bad
луна	[luná]	moon

– М м –

магазин	[magazín]	store / shop
май	[mai]	May
майка	[máyka]	mother
малък	[málăk]	small
мама	[mama]	mommy / mama
март	[mart]	March
маса	[mása]	table
месец	[mésets]	month
месо	[mesó]	meat
мишка	[míška]	mouse
мляко	[mlyáko]	milk
момиче	[momiče]	girl
момче	[momčé]	boy
море	[more]	sea
мъж	[măž]	man

– Н н –

не	[ne]	no
небе	[nebé]	sky
неделя	[nedelya]	Sunday

ноември	[noémvri]	November
нос	[nos]	nose

– O o –

облекло	[oblekló]	clothing
обувка	[obuvka]	shoe
обяд	[obyád]	lunch
огън	[ógăn]	fire
око	[okó]	eye
октомври	[oktomvri]	October
осем	[ósem]	eight

– П п –

пазар	[pazár]	market
панталони	[pantaloni]	pants
парк	[park]	park
пет	[pet]	five
петък	[petăk]	Friday
планина	[planiná]	mountain
понеделник	[ponedelnik]	Monday
приятел	[priyátel]	friend
прозорец	[prozórets]	window
птица	[ptítsa]	bird

– Р р –

река	[reká]	river
ресторант	[restorant]	restaurant
риба	[ríba]	fish

риза	[ríza]	shirt
рокля	[róklya]	dress
ръка	[răká]	hand / arm

– C с –

самолет	[samolét]	airplane
свиня	[svinyá]	pig
седем	[sedem]	seven
септември	[septémvri]	September
сестра	[sestrá]	sister
син	[sin]	blue
син	[sin]	son
сирене	[sírene]	cheese
скъп	[skăp]	expensive
слънце	[slăntse]	sun
сняг	[snyag]	snow
София	[sofíya]	Sofia
сряда	[sryáda]	Wednesday
стол	[stol]	chair
студен	[student]	cold
събота	[săbota]	Saturday
сърце	[sărtsé]	heart

– T т –

татко	[tátko]	daddy / papa
три	[tri]	three
тъжен	[tăžen]	sad
тяло	[tyálo]	body

– У у –

улица	[ulitsa]	street
университет	[universitét]	university
уста	[ustá]	mouth
утре	[utre]	tomorrow
ухо	[ukhó]	ear
училище	[učílište]	school

– Ф ф –

февруари	[fevruari]	February

– Х х –

хляб	[khlyab]	bread
хотел	[khotel]	hotel
храна	[khraná]	food

– Ц ц –

цвят	[tsvyat]	color
цвят	[tsvyat]	flower
църква	[tsărkva]	church

– Ч ч –

чай	[čai]	tea
час	[čas]	hour
червен	[červén]	red

черен	[čéren]	black
четвъртък	[četvărtăk]	Thursday
четири	[čétiri]	four
човек	[covék]	person

– Ш ш –

шапка	[šápka]	hat
шест	[šest]	six

– Щ щ –

щастлив	[štastlív]	happy

– Ю ю –

юли	[yúli]	July
юни	[yúni]	June

– Я я –

ябълка	[yabălka]	apple
януари	[yanuari]	January

Other language learning titles available from Wolfedale Press:

Learn to Read Arabic in 5 Days
Learn to Read Armenian in 5 Days
Learn to Read Georgian in 5 Days
Learn to Read Greek in 5 Days
Learn to Read Modern Hebrew in 5 Days
Learn to Read Persian (Farsi) in 5 Days
Learn to Read Russian in 5 Days
Learn to Read Ukrainian in 5 Days